12 Days of Diwali

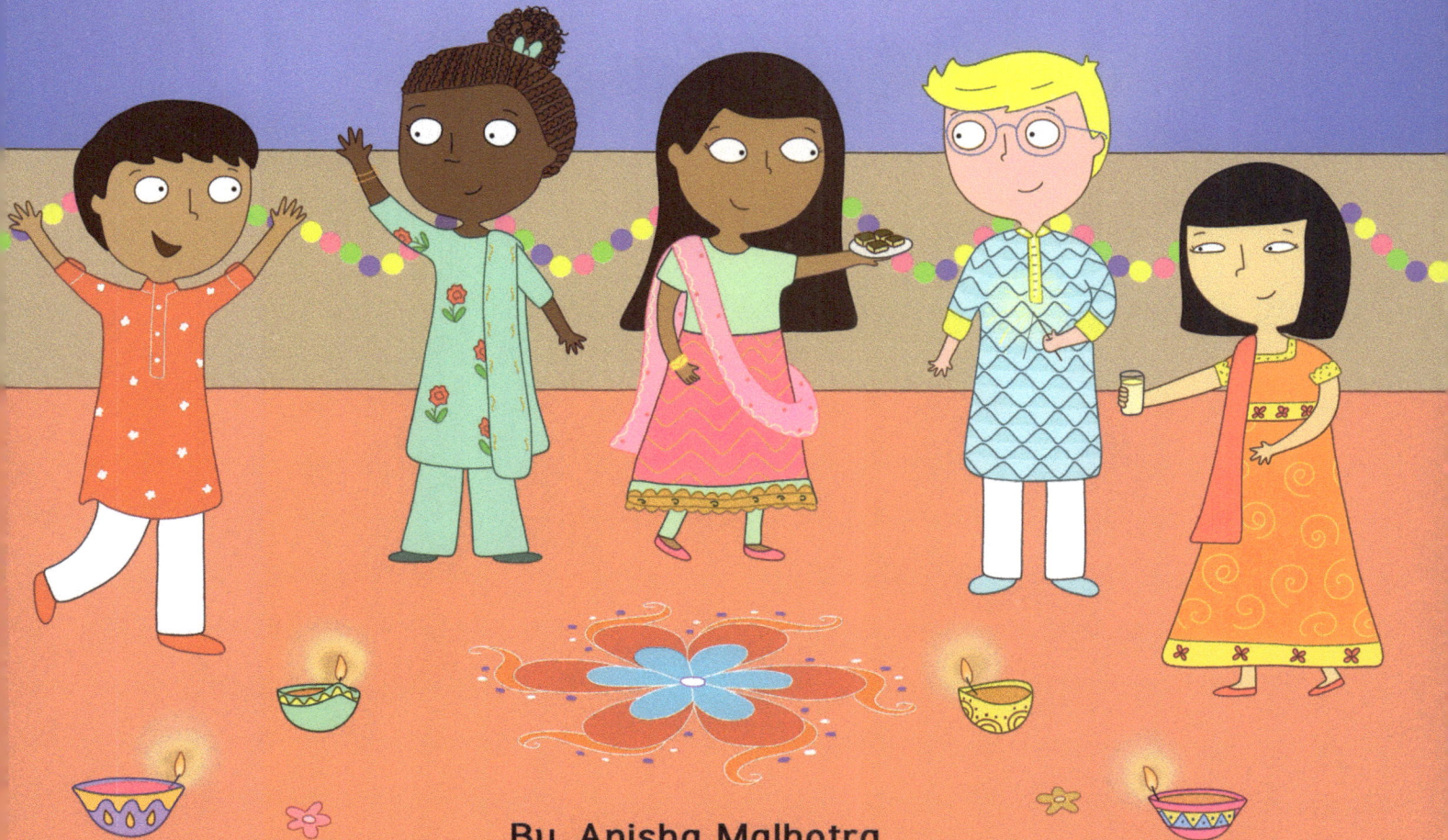

By Anisha Malhotra

Illustrated by Michelle McGovern

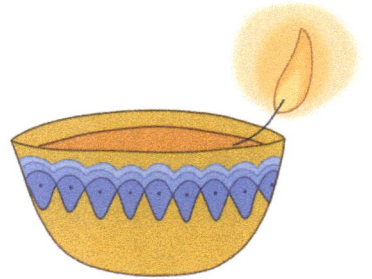

Diwali is a Hindu festival which originates in India. Hinduism is the main religion in India and Diwali is celebrated by over one billion people all over the world.

Diwali is known as the festival of lights and usually occurs in mid October – mid November. The mythological story is about the God Lord Rama defeating the evil demon Ravana in a triumph of good over evil. It is a time of celebration, joy, lights, fireworks, laughter and good food.

This book is designed to help people especially children relate to the cultural elements of Diwali. The most common symbol associated with Diwali is a diya lamp. A small burning candle light. On that note I hope you enjoy this book and may your Diwali be filled with love and joy.

For K, K and S and
the amazing Sawhney Family

First published in the United Kingdom in 2020 by
The Cloister House Press

ISBN 978-1-913460-20-4

On the first day of Diwali my best friend gave to me,
a giant glass of lassi.

On the **second** day of Diwali my best friend gave to me,
two silk shirts
and a giant glass of lassi.

On the third day of Diwali my best friend gave to me,
three hot samosas,
two silk shirts and a giant glass of lassi.

On the fourth day of Diwali my best friend gave to me,
four fire crackers,
three hot samosas, two silk shirts and a giant glass of lassi.

On the fifth day of Diwali my best friend gave to me,
five diya lamps,
four fire crackers, three hot samosas, two silk shirts and a giant glass
of lassi.

On the sixth day of Diwali my best friend gave to me,
six tiny bells,
five diya lamps, four fire crackers, three hot samosas, two silk shirts
and a giant glass of lassi.

On the seventh day of Diwali my best friend gave to me, seven coloured bangles,
six tiny bells, five diya lamps, four fire crackers, three hot samosas, two silk
shirts and a giant glass of lassi.

On the eighth day of Diwali my best friend gave to me,
eight rangoli patterns,
seven coloured bangles, six tiny bells, five diya lamps, four fire crackers,
three hot samosas, two silk shirts and a giant glass of lassi.

On the ninth day of Diwali my best friend gave to me,
nine giant ladoos,
eight rangoli patterns, seven coloured bangles, six tiny bells, five diya lamps,
four fire crackers, three hot samosas, two silk shirts and a giant glass of lassi.

On the tenth day of Diwali my best friend gave to me,
ten chocolate barfis,
nine giant ladoos, eight rangoli patterns, seven coloured bangles, six tiny bells, five diya lamps, four fire crackers, three hot samosas, two silk shirts and a giant glass of lassi.

On the eleventh day of Diwali my best friend gave to me,
eleven silver coins,
ten chocolate barfis, nine giant ladoos, eight rangoli patterns, seven coloured
bangles, six tiny bells, five diya lamps, four fire crackers, three hot samosas,
two silk shirts and a giant glass of lassi.

On the twelfth day of Diwali my best friend gave to me,
twelve dhol players,
eleven silver coins, ten chocolate barfis, nine giant ladoos, eight rangoli patterns, seven coloured bangles, six tiny bells, five diya lamps, four fire crackers, three hot samosas, two silk shirts and a giant glass of lassi.

Glossary

Barfi : Sweet milk cake

Dhol : Drums

Diya : Lamp

Ladoo : A sweet dessert in a ball shape made from flour, sugar and butter

Lassi : A sweet milk drink

Rangoli : Colourful patterns created on the floor using coloured sand, rice or flour.

www.ingramcontent.com/pod-product-compliance
Lightning Source LLC
Chambersburg PA
CBHW041435040426
42452CB00023B/2988